A Special "Gift" for:

_____

This book is lovingly dedicated to
Gramma and Nana
for embracing our children
as only a Grandma could

You're Going to be a GRANDMA!

Written by Deborah L. Zupancic

Illustrated by Joel Grothaus

REVEAL PUBLISHING

Detroit

Text and illustrations Copyright © 2009 Deborah Zupancic All Rights Reserved.

Published by Reveal Publishing.

No part of this publication may be reproduced in whole or in part, or stored in a retrieval system, or transmitted in any form or by any means, electronic, mechanical, photocopying, recording, scanning, or otherwise, without the prior written permission of the publisher. Requests to publisher for permission should be addressed to Permissions Department, Reveal Publishing, 2749 Pendleton Drive, Bloomfield Hills, MI 48304 or by e-mail at permissions@Reveal-Group.com

ISBN: 978-0-9841590-0-0

The Reveal Publishing logo is a trademark of Reveal Publishing.

10 9 8 7 6 5 4 3 2 1

Printed in the U.S.A.

First printing, March 2010

A special thanks to Jeff - my husband, friend, business partner and soul mate.
Without you, I never would have had the courage to make this dream come true.

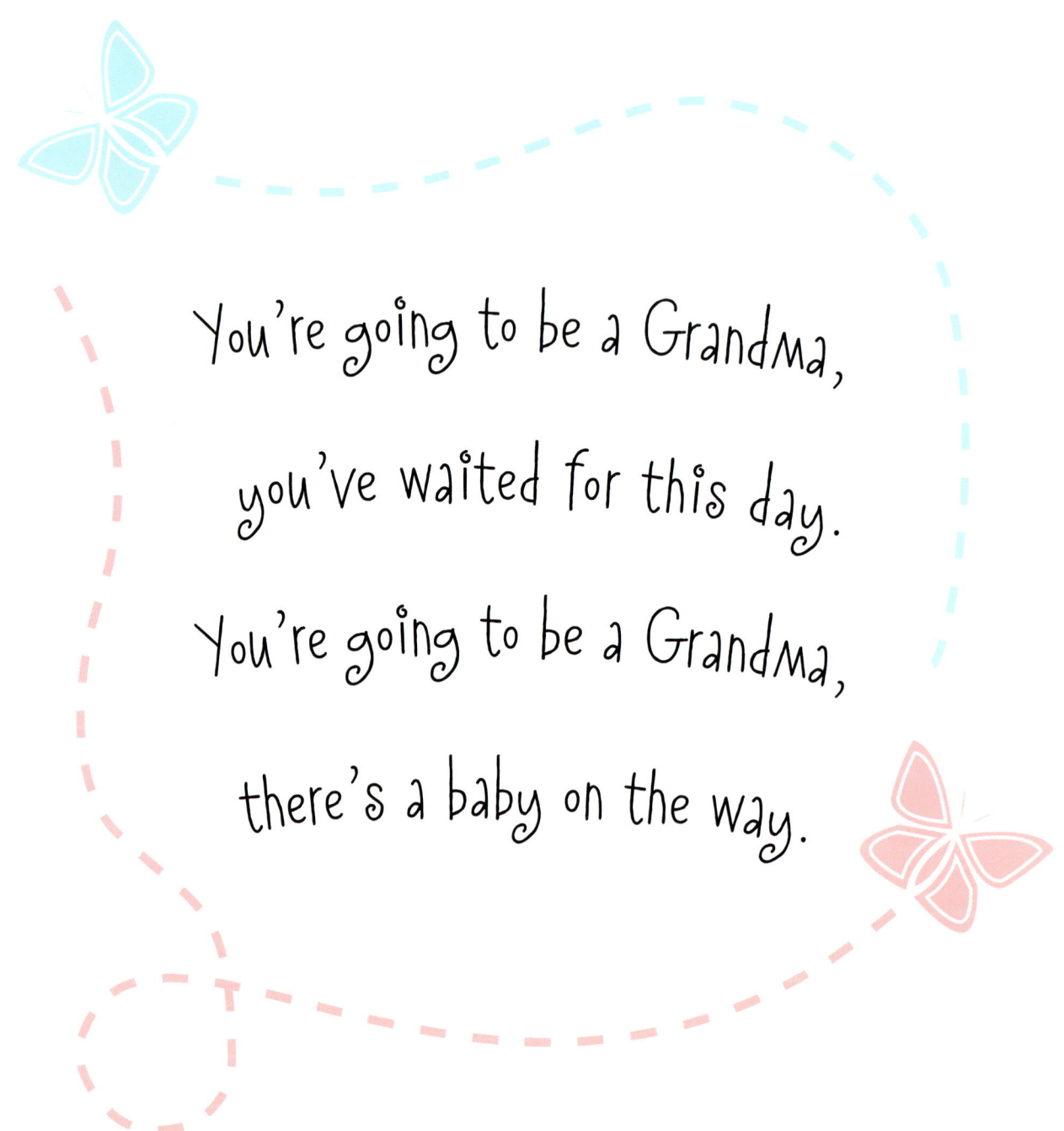

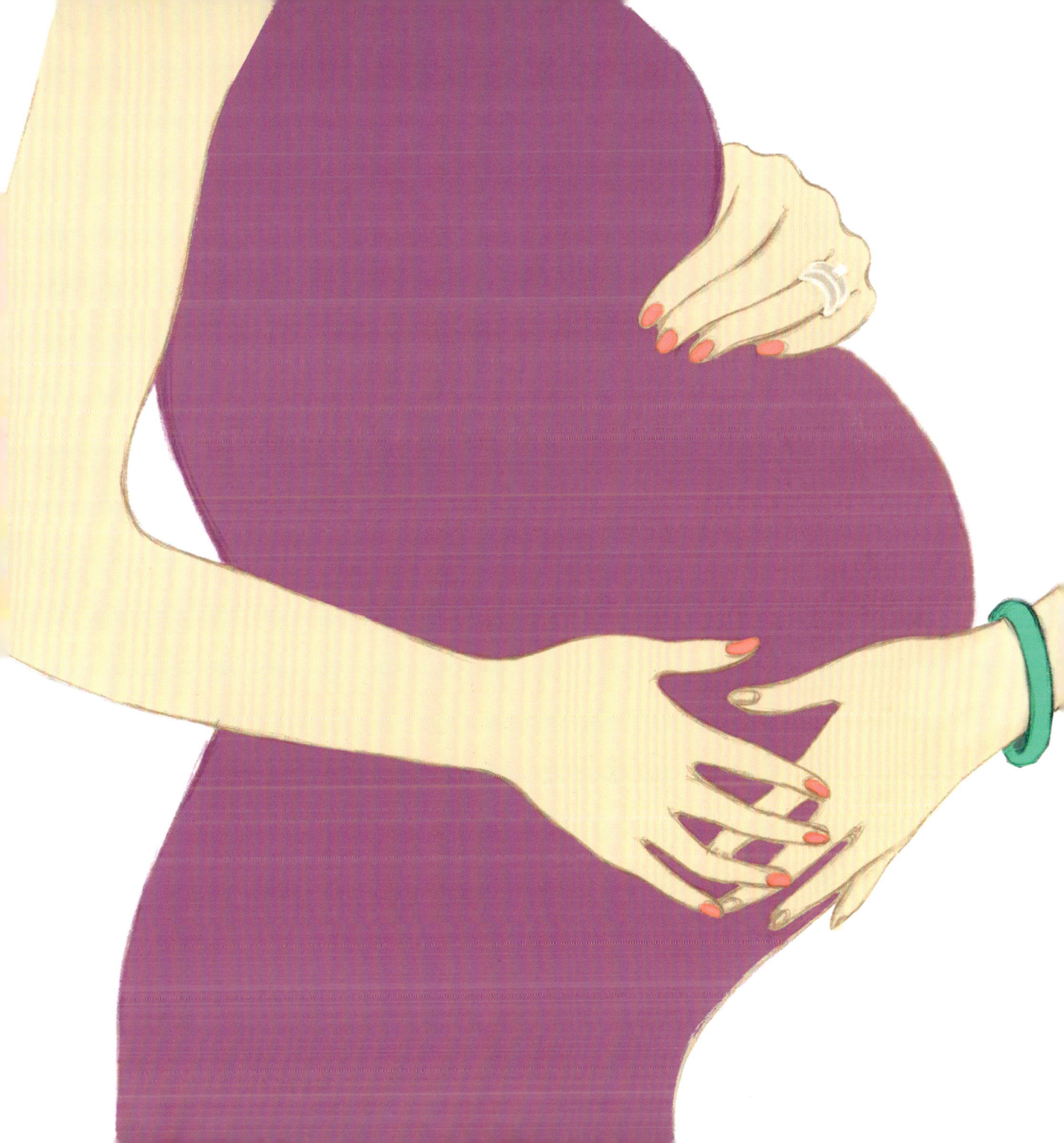

A little one to rock and hold,
to spoil and to love.

A little piece of Heaven,
a blessing from above.

It seems like only yesterday, you had a baby of your own.

The years have passed, how time f l i e s,

Your prayers have now been answered,
a new chapter has begun.

It won't be long before this blessing

 makes its grand debut.

With a loving place inside the heart,

held especially for you.

For babies have a way of knowing

how to seek and find

That special place in Grandma's arms,

so gentle and so kind.

A Grandma comes with insight,

Learning things from long ago.

Ten tiny toes and fingers

don't stay small for long, you know.

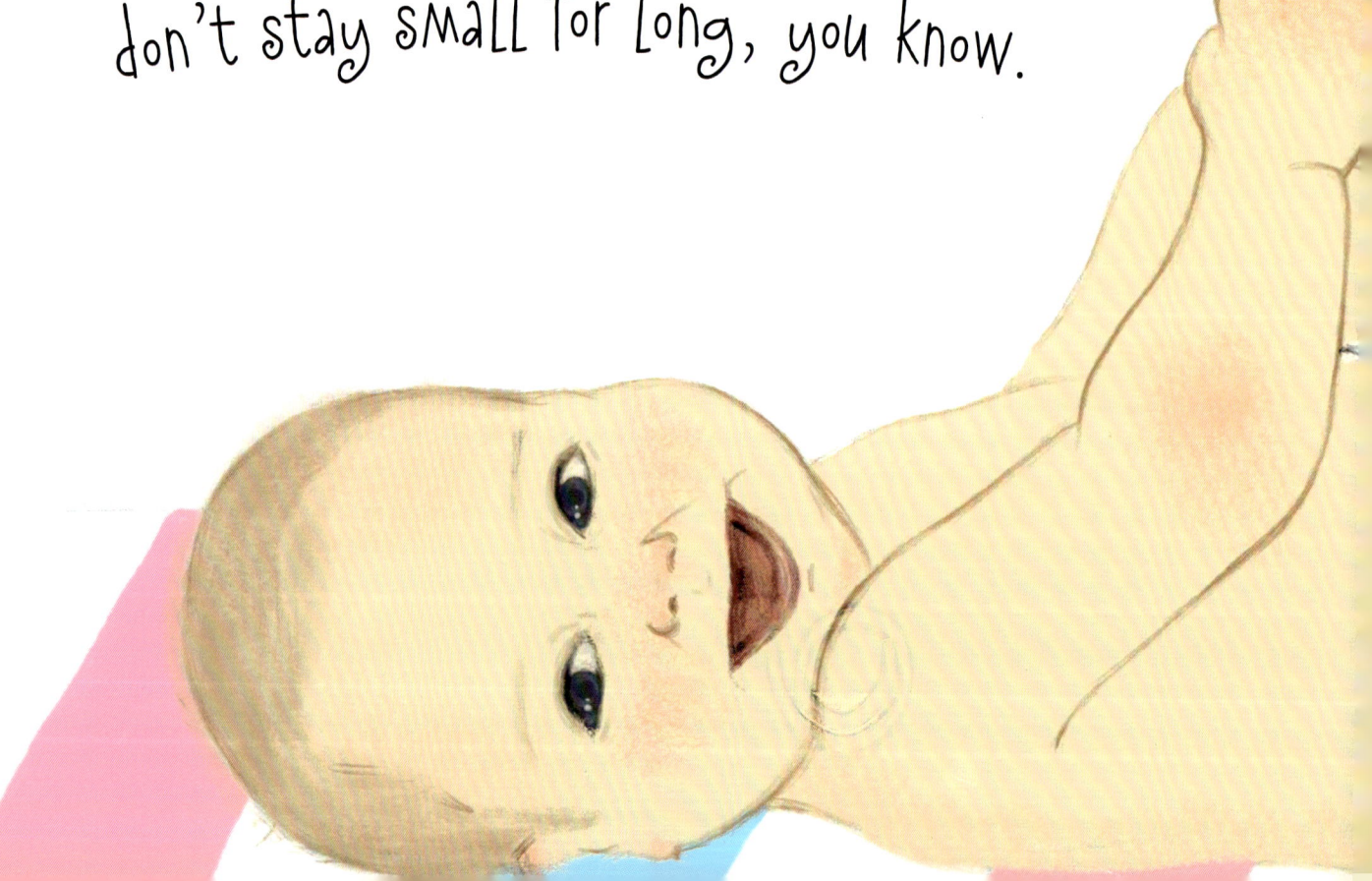

For there's such a small amount of time to hold that tiny hand.

A lesson only Grandmas know, and truly understand.

Cherishing the love you feel, so endless and so deep.

Endless hugs and kisses,
sharing smiles from the heart.

A love that's unconditional,
setting Grandma's love apart.

There is a special benefit, that only Grandmas hold.
It's known throughout the ages,
by Grandmas young and old.

It's spoiling your little one,
baking cookies - buying toys.
Send them back to Mom and Dad,
then quiet you'll enjoy.

Now you can teach your wisdom,

all you've learned along the way.

Your legacy continues,

growing stronger every day.

The family traditions now live on,

the torch will soon be passed.

A little piece of you shines bright,

for this you're truly blessed.

A new chapter in your storybook,

you've waited for this day.

You're going to be a Grandma,

there's a baby on the way.

A little one to rock and hold,

to spoil and to love.

A little piece of Heaven,

a blessing from above.

Baby's Name _____

Day and Date of Birth _____

Time of Birth _____

Weight and Length _____

Eye Color _____

Hair Color _____

Nicknames _____

Distinguishing Characteristics _____

_____

_____

First Impressions_____

_____

_____

About the Author

When she was pregnant with her first child, Deborah Zupancic created a heart-warming poem for her mother to share the good news.
It has now blossomed into this keepsake version for grandmothers everywhere, honoring the unbreakable bond between a grandmother and her grandchildren. Deborah, her husband and their three boys live in Bloomfield Hills, Michigan.

The Joyous Moment: Tell Us Your Story

How did you find out you were going to be a grandma?

Did you receive a special gift?

If you were expecting, how did you tell the grandma-to-be?

Did your share an ultrasound image?

Or did this book announce the big news?

If you have a magical or memorable story to share,
we'd love to hear it — whether it was your first grandchild or your tenth.

Just log on to THEGrandmaBook.com to share your story.

We'd Love to Hear from You:

If you enjoyed this book, please share your comments with us by sending us an e-mail or a letter:

GrandmaBook@Reveal-Group.com

Book Feedback

Reveal Publishing

2749 Pendleton Drive

Bloomfield Hills, MI 48304

THEGrandmaBook.com